The Laughing Postman

&

The Laughing Postman Delivers

True Stories by a Mail Carrier

Dee B. Myrick

*To Mary Turner
Dee Mill
2016
National Rural
Letter Convention*

Dee B. Myrick email: thelaughingpostman@gmail.com

Cover credit: Dee B. Myrick

Editor: Conna Craig (connacraig@gmail.com)

Printed in the United States of America

July 2015

Dedications

To my father, Vernon B. Bunnell. He has always believed in me.

To Mitch for his words of wisdom and for seeing the humor in almost everything.

To George for explaining that the way to friendship with angry dogs is through their stomachs.

To Juanita for being right about the importance of skin lotion. And comfortable vehicles.

To Bobby because tomorrow hasn't been touched yet.

Table of Contents

DEE B. MYRICK

VOLUME ONE. THE LAUGHING POSTMAN

Introduction

We are mothers and fathers. And sons and daughters. Who every day go about our lives with duty, honor and pride. Neither snow, nor rain, nor heat, nor gloom of night, nor the winds of change, nor a nation challenged will stay us from the swift completion of our appointed rounds. Ever.

–United States Postal Service

I am a third-generation postal employee. I deliver mail under all weather conditions. I also deliver mail when I am sick, tired, unhappy, stressed, pregnant, menopausal, and distracted.

Almost every day I have a moment of extreme contentment with my job. It might be in a patch of sunlight shining just so. Or a child's joy about a birthday parcel. A bonneted older lady waving from her garden. A dog wagging its tail. The smell of rain on a hot day. It could be anything or everything.

When that feeling happens, I know that it is a

beautiful day the Lord has made. The intention of this book is to share that feeling.

THE LAUGHING POSTMAN

Part One. Dogs

Dog Bites Sign

In my profession I deal with dogs daily, from Chihuahuas to Dobermans. In this case, the dog is a Dalmatian. He is a beautiful dog, beloved by his owner and treated as if he were a baby. In fact, his name is Baby. He doesn't bite or growl. Never eats or pees on parcels. Great dog, eh? All in all he is wonderfully behaved, but Baby has one bad habit. He chases cars, sometimes for long distances, all the while making an earsplitting high-pitched bark.

One day I was delivering a parcel and had just had enough. Accompanied by the yapping dog as I approached a speed limit sign, I swerved just a little. And Baby swerved just a little. We were going about fifteen miles an hour when it happened. Maybe I expected him to slow down and allow me to get away, or maybe the devil made me do it. Baby hit the sign running at about 15 miles per hour. I looked back, no barking, no dog. He was lying very still by the sign. I was horrified.

My first thought: *I'd killed a beloved dog!* I backed up and looked down. He was breathing, and didn't have a single mark on him. Baby had just knocked himself out cold.

Baby's house was in sight. I went to the front door and rang the doorbell. His owner, a very nice woman, answered the door. She took one look at my face and said: "You've run over my dog!"

"Not exactly," I replied, stepping back and pointing to the prone dog. "He ran into the sign." Baby was just fine and he'd learned his lesson; he never chased cars again. And I never told his owner about my swerve.

Killer Chihuahua

Every occupation has its nightmares. As a rural mail carrier, I have two. One is getting rear-ended while my arm is in a mailbox and the other is getting seriously attacked by dogs. In my nearly thirty years with the postal service, neither has happened, yet.

However, I have been bitten. Anyone who makes regular home deliveries will tell you... it's not the big dogs that worry us. Big dogs can be seen and reasoned with. You can apologize for invading their territory. Big dogs understand the difference between leaving a parcel and stealing something. Little dogs don't care... they just want to KILL.

The dog that bit me escaped its owner when she opened the door to take her parcel. He darted around behind me and bit me on the leg, right above my shoe. And his teeth met. I was hopping around trying to shake the dog loose, while his owner was begging me not to hurt him. She literally had to pry the dog's jaws apart to make him let go.

It took a very long time to heal because every time I took a step, the wound would reopen. And yes... the dog was a Chihuahua.

Boomerang Dog

Mail carriers get to know the dogs on our routes. Partly for self-preservation and also, in most cases, because we see the dogs more than the customers. The postal service, in its infinite wisdom, came out with study findings that showed that if a carrier knew the dog's name, it would be 84% less likely to bite. I cheat and carry dog treats.

My route was almost a hundred miles long and covered three counties in a long loop. At the end of my route was a dog named Arthur who had only three legs. He liked to chase cars and one caught him. One day I was at the far corner of my route when I saw Arthur trotting down the road. He was about twenty miles from home.

I asked him what he was doing so far from home with no collar. He recognized my voice and seemed very happy to see me. What else could I do? I loaded him up, went on with my route and dropped him off at his house. His owners weren't home. About a week later, I saw Arthur at a different part of my route and again gave him a ride home. His owners weren't home that day, either.

I felt pretty good about myself for my Good Samaritan deed, so the next time I saw the owners in their yard, I stopped. I asked how their dog was doing, intending to tell about his journeys. The man looked over at Arthur with a disgusted expression. "I've given him away twice to get rid of him but he keeps coming back. Guess we'll just have to keep him."

I didn't tell him about my special deliveries. Arthur grinned and wagged his tail.

Sassy and the Kittens

Sassy was a dog on my route, a large dog, part bulldog and cur, with some grizzly bear somewhere in her lineage. She scared me. She was one of those dogs that, when she growled, every sharp tooth in her mouth showed. I did not get out of my truck at that address.

Sassy lived at the end of a long one-lane road, enclosed by heavily forested land. Her owner was an elderly woman living alone. She loved and needed that dog for companionship and protection. She was active in her church and often traveled.

It was check day; I knew Sassy's owner would be gone, but that she would get her check and take it to the bank later. (This was before direct deposit.) I headed down the driveway and had just made the turn into the drive when I saw the kittens. There were three tiny, barely-able-to-walk kittens. They were in the middle of the road.

I had three options: run over the kittens... not happening; go around and get stuck in the yard; or get out and get eaten by the bear dog. Delivering the check was important. I pondered this and tried to figure out a solution.

Sassy was doing her thing, growling, showing her fangs and seeing how high her hair could stand up. Then she stopped. She looked at me, she looked at the kittens, and she looked at the mailbox. Then she did the most amazing thing.

The 85-pound, bulldog-cur-bear of a dog picked up a kitten very gently in her mouth and moved it out of the road. I watched, stunned, as she repeated this feat two more times. Then Sassy resumed threatening my life.

Sassy has a head full of sense and a heart of gold... but I still don't get out of my truck when she's around.

Flatfooted

I was running my route in a small car. My method of serving mailboxes is to have the mail for the box in hand, pull up to the box, flag down, lid down, box open, mail in, hand out, lid up. Then I look down and get the mail for the next box in hand before I pull away.

One day, when I looked back up before going forward, I was nose to nose with a very large dog. I froze. The dog, a Great Dane, shifted and leaned forward until his head was inside the car. He looked at the empty driver's seat. I leaned out the window to see what the dog was standing on. He was so large that he was standing flatfooted outside my car.

I leaned back into the car as he pulled out. He sat down and cocked his head at me in doggy inquiry. I just shrugged. His name was Harley and we became good friends.

Part Two. Customers

Power of the Grandmother

I had delivered a particular route for twelve years. Near a park was a cluster of mailboxes in a long row. I would serve a box, let up on the brake, coast to the next box and serve it. Four young men decided to entertain themselves by harassing me.

I tried ignoring them. They were in their late teens and early twenties, with baggy pants, gang headscarves and foul mouths. The language became crude and rude. At the last box I made eye contact with the ringleader. "J.J.," I said, "I'll be by this afternoon to talk to Mrs. H."

J.J. was about to spew more trash but his mouth shut with an audible click. He paled. I felt a little sorry for him. "Might go easier for you if you talk to her first." It's hard to be afraid of someone you coached in free throws when he was six years old.

When I reached Mrs. H she was sitting on her

porch in a rocking chair, leisurely waving a funeral home fan. I got out and took the mail up. The young men came out of the house. What a difference! The headgear was gone and the hair neat. Pants had belts and the shirts were tucked in.

They stood in front of me and each one apologized for his actions, disrespect and bad language. I looked at Mrs. H. She said, "Will that do?" I nodded, neither of us smiled.

Never, never underestimate the power of a grandmother.

No Safe Drivers

A "box holder" is a piece of mail delivered to every mailbox on a route, usually without a name or address. An "addressed box holder" is one that has the individual address but no names. "Current resident" means the sender intends the mail to go to anyone who lives there currently.

I delivered a set of addressed box holders from a vehicle insurance company. They were addressed to the safe driver at that address. I delivered 672 safe driver advertisements on a Tuesday.

On Wednesday, I picked up over fifty pieces of the safe driver mail with variations written on them of "No such person here."

Payday Express

At one time, my route went up a four-lane highway, made a big loop and ended up back where I started on the other side of the highway. The beginning and ending of my rural route were mostly businesses. I was running early one day and finished up my last box before normal. The secretary smiled when I went in with her company's normal Friday Express Mail.

"The boss said we could go home as soon as you came with the payroll," she explained.

The next Friday, I had their Express but I was not early. I looked across the highway at the business on the end of my route. I crossed the road and delivered their mail four hours early. The secretary laughed when I asked if they could go home.

They were great customers and gave the postal service all their business.

Purple Polka Dots

I was working a seriously overburdened mail route. This route averaged around seven thousand pieces of mail a day, six days a week. It was one of those hot, humid summer days.

While I was working at a set of mailboxes, a young lady stepped out of her air-conditioned apartment and approached me. She had mailed a letter to a friend last week, and did I remember what day that was? I just stared at her.

I told her I handled thousands of pieces of mail every day. And the only way I would remember a single letter would be if it had purple polka dots all over it. She laughed.

For the next three years I delivered mail to that address. Every piece of mail she sent was covered with purple polka dots.

Sweet Apologies

I am a mail carrier in hurricane country. During Hurricane Katrina, almost every house on my route was affected. Blue tarps covered most of the homes and roofing companies came from other states to help out. Debris from trees, power lines, houses and outbuildings covered the roads.

I was constantly getting flat tires. Wires, nails and tree limbs were puncturing my tires. At one point, I had 27 nails in four tires. I bought an extra spare tire and a really good jack. I replaced six tires before all the mess was cleared. But the medicines, checks, insurance information, and letters from family that I had to deliver were important.

As time went on, tempers flared over the lack of electricity (it was hot!), shortages at the stores, and the insurance companies dragging their feet.

One day a lady met me at her box and proceeded

to yell and cuss at me. I learned new words that day. Her insurance company told her they had mailed her check the week before and what the heck had I done with it?

I had not had a good week. No ice, no hot water, three flat tires, cold meals... I was not a happy camper. I told the lady I delivered every piece of mail I received every day, that she would get her damn (yes I cussed back) letter the day I did. She stomped away. A week later her letter came. I was still upset over her treatment of me, so I circled the postmark and drew six arrows toward it. She never said a word.

Several weeks later I stopped at a store on my route and the cussing customer was there. We didn't speak. When I got to her box the flag was up and there were two of my favorite candy bars inside. I found out later she had asked the store clerk what I liked. I accepted her apology and ate the candy.

AKA Bookmobile

Occasionally people will be waiting at the mailbox when we deliver. During the summer, the people waiting are often kids. One day, a polite young man of about nine years old was waiting for me, but he wasn't interested in the mail. He wanted to know if a bookmobile came to the area. I sadly informed him that it did not.

The public library had been an important part of my life and I was sorry to see that service stopped. The boy was about the same age as my son so I asked him what he liked to read. He said *Animorphs* and *Goosebumps*. Those were the same books my son was reading.

I had always encouraged my children to read. When we went to the store, if they wanted toys or candy I said no; if they wanted books, I always, always said yes. As a result we had lots and lots of books in my home.

I told the disappointed boy that if his mother would write me a note giving permission, I would leave a book in his mailbox. When he returned it I would leave another.

Over the summer he read all of my son's books and more. Sometimes he would wait for me at the box to talk to me. I looked forward to that part of my route, and when he wasn't there I was disappointed.

One day, another customer, an adult, was waiting by the box with him and said, "Hi, Mail Lady!"

The boy said, "That's not the mail lady... she's the bookmobile."

Emergency Not

What constitutes an emergency is open to interpretation. My mother told us as kids that if blood wasn't spurting, not to bother her. When I cut my foot bad enough to spurt, she made me hold my foot out the window of the car on the way to the doctor so I wouldn't get blood in the car.

Part of my route covered a gated community with a large lake, wooded areas and a golf course with trails crisscrossing it. It is a beautiful neighborhood. As I rounded a curve, three preteen boys waved me down. They were out of breath, red faced and frightened. "It's an emergency!"

Adrenalin surged as possibilities ran through my mind. Drowning, fire, broken bones, blood spurting. I was instantly prepared to leap into action.

And then reality.

"Our golf cart battery died and we gotta get it

home before Dad finds out we drove it."

I told them to deal with it, and drove on.

Karate, Judo and Other Words

My grandmother was a tiny woman who did not know the meaning of fear. I was with her one time when she cut off another driver in order to get a good parking space. The other driver was a very angry, very large man. As he approached my grandmother, she took a karate stance and informed him that she knew karate, judo, and "other words just like that." He turned and walked away. She grinned at me and said, "And I have a brick in my purse."

I had a group of apartment mailboxes that I had to get out of my truck to serve. One of my customers began waiting for me. He seemed a little too friendly. I made sure to mention my husband. He didn't seem to care.

As time went on, he got uncomfortably pushy. I mentioned my husband was in the Army. The man asked what he did. I quickly flashed back to my now deceased grandmother. I told him my husband was a karate instructor, and proudly boasted that I was his best student. I never saw the man again.

BR-549

A farmer on my route bought himself a used (very used) bulldozer. He told me that he spent more time working on it than using it. One day, he was cleaning up some storm downed trees beside the road when it broke down the last time. And there it sat. He said it could rust to nothing for all he cared because he was done.

After a couple of years, some wit put a sign on the piece of junk bulldozer that gave me a laugh. One day I saw a car pulled off by it and a young man waved me over.

He wasn't from around here, he told me, and asked if could I explain something. "Is the number on the For Sale sign a local phone number of some kind?" he asked, because his cell phone couldn't reach it.

I asked him if he'd ever heard of Junior Sample

and the television show Hee-Haw. BR-549. And yes, I know this dates me.

Birthday Surprise

When there are a lot of cars at a customer's home it is usually one of two things—a death in the family or a birthday party. On this day I could tell it was a birthday, because I had a parcel to deliver that had "Happy Birthday from Grandma and Grandpa" written in large, colorful letters.

It was noisy in the house so it was several minutes before someone answered the door. I was greeted with enthusiasm and the mom started to take the parcel. She hesitated, and then asked if I would give it to her daughter. I followed the mom through the house to the birthday party-themed backyard.

There were princess-themed balloons, streamers, and a jumpy house. It was an eight-year-old girl's dream birthday party. The children were sitting at a long table with the birthday girl at the head. They had striped, pointed hats on and were eating cake. When I walked up with the parcel all eyes turned to me. Inspired, I said in an official voice, "I am from the United States Post Office, and I have a very important parcel, all the way from California for a Miss Amy."

Amy raised her hand and I put the parcel on the table in front of her. She looked up at me and asked if she would have to sign for it. The parcel didn't require a signature. However, I told her, "All important parcels have to be signed for." I whipped out a pen and the signature slip from my pocket. The other children watched, wide eyed, as Amy signed her name.

Her mom told me later that my delivery was the highlight of the party.

Nice Ice

This was one of the nicest things a customer ever did for me. It was one of the hottest summers on record, and the news was posting continuous heat advisories. There is no air conditioning in postal jeeps. We can't use the air conditioner in our private vehicles because it makes the engines run hot. To survive this weather, I would wet down a towel and wrap it around my head and shoulders. Within a few minutes, the towel and my hair would be totally dry again. It is common for mail carriers to suffer from heat strokes.

I was so hot that day that I had a headache, muscle cramps, and was slightly nauseated. I was seriously in danger of becoming overheated. I had started the route with cold water, but it was warm now. The flag was up at the box and I was surprised to find not outgoing mail, but a tinfoil wrapped glass goblet, a frozen sports drink and a note that read, "ENJOY!"

The goblet had ice and two small Snickers candy bars, frozen. The sports drink had been partially frozen and was very, very cold. I did enjoy the treat. And the thoughtfulness of my customer touched my heart.

Postal Food Drive

Every year the United States Postal Service sponsors a nationwide food drive on the second Saturday of May. Customers are asked to put nonperishable food items in a bag on or near the mailbox. All the food collected in the community stays in that community. Local food banks pick up the food the same day it is collected.

One year, several weeks after the food drive, one of my customers asked if she could maybe have some of that "Post Office food." Seems she had been sick and had to choose between medicine and food. She just needed a little, she said, until the end of the month. She was a proud elderly woman I liked and I enjoyed visiting with her. I could see that it bothered her to ask. I said I would check.

Of course the food bank supplies had been turned in already, so when I picked up my kids after work we went to the store and bought the lady groceries. They enjoyed the idea of helping her. I used that opportunity to teach them what my grandmother had taught me: having enough that you can afford to give some away is the best feeling in the world. Not having enough so you have to accept some is the worst feeling in the world. And it is always best to give anonymously.

So I let the lady think it was food from the food drive. That would have been the end of it except the lady called my postmaster to thank him. He told her that the food drive was over and that I had given her the food. She never spoke to me again.

Part Three. Weird Mail

The Great Bee Escape

Sometimes we have unusual items to deliver. A frantic clerk asked if any of the carriers knew anything about honeybees. I did, so I was led to the parcel sorting area. A medium size wire caged box was swarming with honeybees, all on the outside of the container.

The clerk told me a hole had been punctured on the side of the box and the bees poured out. The clerks had vacated one side of the building and operation of the post office had shut down. They wanted me to scoop the parcel into a garbage bag. Someone had gone to get the wasp spray.

They wanted to kill the honeybees! The customer who had ordered these bees had probably waited months, as the demand is high in the beekeeping world. "No, no," I said.

Using only my bare hand, I began herding the

bees back into the box through the hole. The clerk gasped, but I explained that the queen was in a separate box inside the cage and her workers would not abandon her. The bees were in swarm mode and would not sting because they didn't have a hive to protect.

We taped the hole shut and the customer was notified. Postal operations resumed and I was the hero of the day.

Bubbles

When a national laundry detergent company added a new liquid product to their line, they sent samples through the mail. Lots and lots of samples. For my route that meant over six hundred packages. I had a small car at the time and dumped the samples into the backseat and floorboard on top of the mail. Some of the little packages were sticky, but I didn't think anything of it.

Then it began to rain, not a drizzle but a gully wash. Let's just say I had very clean mail that day.

Pig Sticker

One of the weirdest things I've ever had to deliver was a spear. At this time in my rural carrier career, I was driving a small four-door Honda. This posed a logistical problem, as the spear was almost as long as the car. It wasn't going to fit in the trunk or in the back seat. Someone suggested I call the customer to come to the office to get his parcel. Not happening. This was my job.

I rolled down the windows on the driver's side, both front and back. By weaving the flexible spear shaft in one window and out the other, I threaded it the length of my car. I taped the spear to the side mirror. I drove the car from the passenger seat.

The pointy end stuck out a little from the front of the car. The customer was surprised to see me bringing his parcel. It was a hog-hunting spear, he told me. He had expected to have to go to the post office to pick it up.

The customer with the spear lived in the middle of my route. I still smile when I remember some of the looks I got from other drivers.

Ghost at the Post Office

My father was the officer-in-charge in a small-town post office. When a special delivery package arrived that he knew was eagerly awaited, he called the customer. The workers in the post office asked what was in the vase. My father told them it was the cremated remains of a person.

Upon hearing this, three of the five people working in the office vacated the building and refused to return until the urn was gone.

THE LAUGHING POSTMAN

Part Four. Embarrassing

Moments

In My Face

I am a country girl. Part of my route was a very wealthy gated community. I watched this area being developed from forestland and cow pastures, from five mailboxes to two hundred. It was awesome seeing half-million dollar houses with fancy landscaping built before my eyes.

One day as I was serving the boxes, I heard a weird sound. It was a whizz-pop-swish sound. I heard it again and again. I looked around, worried that a new kind of wasp was about to attack. There it was again, right beside my truck. I looked down to see something coming out of the ground. It was metallic and round. I leaned out to get a closer look. *Whizz* was the round metal thing rising from the ground. *Pop* was something opening. *Swish* was the cold water hitting me in the face. That was my first experience with automatic underground sprinkler

systems.

The Naked Truth

When I first started as a mail carrier, my coworkers filled my ears with unbelievable stories. Dogs climbing in the windows, naked people answering the doors, being invited for big country lunches and many more. As a naïve twenty-year-old, I thought they were pulling my leg.

In my second month working, I had a large parcel requiring a signature for delivery. I pulled up in the driveway, got out and started to ring the doorbell. A totally naked man with a big grin opened the door. The surprise on his face must have mirrored mine. He slammed the door. After a shocked moment he yelled through the door, "Who are you?"

"I'm the mail lady," I answered. "I have a parcel that needs a signature."

He told me to wait a minute. The next time the door opened he was wearing a large towel. He was expecting someone else he explained, red faced, as he signed for the parcel.

As I pulled out of the driveway someone else pulled in. She gave me a cheery wave.

Turns out none of the tales my coworkers told me were lies. But those are for a different day.

Holidays

At times in my thirty years as a rural mail carrier, I have worked overburdened routes six days a week. A normal route is between forty-eight and fifty-four hours with one day off, usually Saturday. I have worked seventy-two hour routes with no day off when the post office was short-handed, for over a year. I was very, very tired.

My usual routine is to get up by five, get ready and drive an hour, with a stop for gas. Some days I would get something for breakfast before getting to the post office where I would work on my feet for three hours, ride my route for five hours, with frequent dismounts, before going back to the post office to turn in and head back home and be off on Saturdays. On an overburdened route, I would work on my feet for six hours, run the route for eight hours... even on Saturdays.

I felt like the Dunkin' Donut Man, and would meet myself coming and going. I was leaving for work in the dark and coming home in the dark. My husband was sometimes supportive and sometimes not. Mostly I left him sleeping when I left for work, and fell into bed exhausted every night. I was bone tired.

It was one of those times when I went to work as usual, leaving my husband asleep in bed. I had driven an hour to work and was putting gas in my truck when my husband called. He almost never called this early. He wanted to know where I was...

I told him.

He told me that it was a holiday, and that the post office was closed. I drove by the post office anyway, just to make sure, and later we laughed about it.

Arrested Delivery

I was delivering the mail on a high-traffic road when a county sheriff pulled into a driveway ahead of me. The officer was waiting at the mailbox. He wanted me to hand over the customer's mail. I said no. He puffed up and demanded the mail. I told him that only a postmaster or a postal inspector could see someone's mail. He said it was official business and that I was interfering with an investigation. He was angry but I knew my job. He went back to his car and I continued my route.

I hadn't driven far before the officer was behind me with his lights on. Now this was before cell phones and I was getting worried. He made me get out and put my hands on my truck. He searched me for weapons. I was so embarrassed. People, my customers, where driving by seeing this. He asked me if I was ready to give him the mail. I said no!

He was very angry and had his hand on his gun. I was frightened. He made me wait while he talked to someone on his radio. He came back, red-faced and tight-lipped. He said I could go.

When I got back to my office my postmaster was waiting for me. *What if I was wrong?* I would be fired. The postmaster was angry also and had me tell him exactly what had happened. I was ready to cry, I was so upset.

My boss told me I had done the right thing, and that the sheriff's department would be getting a visit from the postal inspectors. I hoped they gave that County Mounty hell.

Dirty Mail

Mail can be dirty. It gets dusty from transportation, paper fuzz from the sorting machines, and ink. Ink is the worst. "Box holders" are advertising papers that are not addressed, and we place one in each box. The paper is cheap and sometimes the ink isn't completely dry. Add hot humid days, perspiration, and condensation from ice water, and you have the potential for a real mess.

On a particular day, I had a high volume of mail with a set of box holders. That means even if the customer has no addressed mail to deliver or pick up, I have to stop at each box. It adds an hour or more to my day. By the time I loaded my truck I was sweating. I sit on the passenger seat, with the mail in my lap and the box holders in the driver's seat. My left hand grabs the paper and shifts it to my right hand to go into the box.

I had a summer cold with a very itchy nose. A couple of hours into my route I noticed my customers were looking at me funny and smiling. Toward the end of my route I had a delivery to a church that required that I get out of my truck. The secretary laughed when she saw me, and told me to go look in a mirror.

Throughout the day I had rubbed my nose with ink stained fingers. I was now sporting an ink mustache and goatee.

Embarrassing Butterflies

I had a customer who was ordering tube-type parcels—the kind posters, photos and blueprints come in. These parcels required a signature, and as the customers were rarely home I would make the attempt to deliver them in a somewhat leisurely fashion. That means I would drive into the empty carport, blow the horn, get out and ring the doorbell a couple of times, get back in my truck, and leave.

On this particular day, after I rang the doorbell and turned around, I noticed a gigantic spider web in one corner of the garage. Trapped in the web was a huge, brightly colored butterfly. It was still alive, struggling. I was determined to save the butterfly.

I tried jumping to dislodge the web, but I was too short. Being a member of a tool-using species, I used the tube parcel in my attempt to reach the web. But I was still too short. By once again jumping several times I was finally able to reach the web and knock it down, rescuing the struggling butterfly.

I carefully removed the web from the butterfly and opened my hand to release it. The butterfly fluttered away happily. That's when I heard the enthusiastic clapping behind me. The entire family had witnessed the butterfly rescue. Complete with my jumping jacks. What could I do? I took a bow and got the signature for the web-sticky parcel.

Peeing Contest

I would often drive by county road crews on my mail route. On this occasion I came around a sharp curve in a low-traffic area just in time to see three grown men standing in a row peeing. The looks on their faces when they saw me were priceless.

But the funniest thing was when they all tried to spin around to turn their backs to me, they didn't stop peeing... on each other

Part Five. Critters

Great Balls of Snakes

It happened on a curvy, narrow, tree-covered country road. I wasn't going fast, really. Suddenly a giant green wiggly ball dropped on my windshield. The soccer ball-sized clump dissolved into a mass of green snakes. Many, many green snakes.

Driving from the passenger seat with the window down, I hit the brakes hard, and the snakes slid down my hood and out of sight. I immediately slid to a stop, half-on, half-off the road. Maybe three seconds passed.

Except for a new crack in my windshield, there was nothing to prove a great ball of snakes had attacked me that day.

Pecan Dividends

My dad was a mail carrier. One of his customer's mailboxes was attached to its post by crossed nails. That left a space under the door just big enough for a squirrel to stash a pecan during the season. Dad would take the pecan each day and eat it.

It was a hard, cold winter. My dad started feeling guilty about the stolen pecans. He bought some whole pecans at great expense and each day placed one back under the door for the squirrel. I found out about this when he complained that the squirrel had received twice as many pecans as my dad had taken.

Car-surfing Cat

I was delivering to a subdivision that ended in a cul-de-sac. Across the road a garage door slowly opened. I watched closely as the station wagon backed out. I wanted to make sure the driver saw me and didn't back into me. That had happened to other carriers.

She saw me and waved. I started to wave back but was distracted by the hitchhiker on top of the car. The largest Persian cat I had ever seen was sprawled across the top of the station wagon. My return wave became frantic as she backed into the road. I turned around and followed her through the subdivision until she finally noticed me waving mail.

The lady stopped and got out of her car to see what I had for her. I pointed to the top of her car. The cat was having a really bad hair day, but had managed to hang on. The customer thanked me for saving her pet. I laughed and said I had never before seen a car-surfing cat.

Discouraging Turtles

I have always liked turtles. They fascinate me with their reptilian gaze and ever-so-patient forward plodding. When I was a child, my uncles would catch gopher turtles for me when I visited my grandparents. And of course I had aquatic green turtles as pets. I like turtles and I know a little something about them.

A small boy and his grandmother were near their mailbox one day. The boy had a box turtle, and enthusiastically explained that he was going to keep it for a pet. Behind him, his grandmother was rolling her eyes and shaking her head. I told the boy I knew a little about turtles.

He asked what kind of turtle it was. I told him it was a three-toed box turtle and its age. He was impressed. His grandmother just shook her head at me. So I told him all about turtles in general and his turtle in particular. The complicated care and feeding. The sicknesses they get. The sicknesses they give. How expensive veterinary bills can be. The importance of washing his hands every single time he touched the turtle. How sad the turtle would be in a cage. After I told him more than he ever wanted to know, I drove away.

On another day, the grandmother met me without the boy and thanked me for discouraging the pet turtle idea. He had released the turtle.

Bulls

My grandfather was a rural mail carrier like I am. When I visited him, he always wanted to know about how the postal service was changing. We have self-sticking stamps; they had to add glue to stamps in our humid climate. We weigh our parcels at the office; they carried scales. We have more mailboxes, with fewer miles to the route; they had fewer mailboxes and more miles. When I complained about a dog he laughed and slapped his leg. "Dogs! It wasn't dogs we worried about ... it was the bulls."

He told me this story. He had a parcel and was headed for the porch when a bull trotted around the corner of the house. It was closer to his truck than the porch so he took off running. He had barely gotten the door shut when the bull slammed and pushed the truck into a ditch. There my grandfather stayed, cornered by the bull, until the farmer came home for lunch.

The farmer haltered the bull and tied him up. Then he got his tractor and pulled my grandfather out of the ditch. I've had encounters with deer, dogs, birds, snakes, turtles, horses, rats, and irate customers... but never a bull.

Road Kill

One morning, while preparing the mail for our routes, two of my coworkers got into a discussion about road kill. Specifically whether it was o.k. to eat it or not. I was entertained by the country boy's practicality, and the urban dweller's squeamishness.

Later on my route I noticed a patch of fur on the road. Thinking I might test the country boy's convictions, I slowed down to see how fresh it was. I stopped beside the ball of fur and leaned out to take a look. The "road kill" wasn't dead, and it darted under my truck. It didn't come back out.

It was one thing to check out road kill but I had no wish to create any. Putting my truck in park, I opened the door and leaned over to look under. A squirrel-sized red fur ball, but with a pointed face, looked back. I had no idea what kind of animal it was but it wasn't dead, and I didn't want to kill it.

Getting out, I crouched down and looked again. It looked young, whatever it was.

"Here kitty, kitty," I called. And it came. I put the not-kitty in a tub. It just so happened that I had a veterinary clinic at the end of my route, and my mystery was solved. It was a baby ferret, perfectly tame. That was not the end of my story though. I took the fur ball back to the post office and waited for the country boy.

When he came in I showed him the closed tub and informed him it was his supper. Baby ferret had been cooped up for hours by this time. My coworker, expecting something dead, was tentative about opening the tub. He was a good sport though, so he did and when the ferret leaped out the country boy squealed like a two-year-old.

The ferret had an adventurous life with several families, and died of old age.

Squirrel of Justice

There really is justice in the world. Sometimes it's easy to doubt when criminals get off on a technicality or someone less qualified gets your promotion. But I believe there is justice, and good deeds can be rewarded. A squirrel taught me this.

U.S. rural mail carriers who use their own vehicles sit in the passenger seat and drive with their left leg and arm. Seat belts aren't practical because the twisting and turning tightens the belt unbearably. Speeding is frowned on by law enforcement, but speeding with no one in the driver's seat is especially bad.

One day, I was running late. My son had a ball game that afternoon, and there was a long stretch of road with no mailboxes and only a couple of abandoned barns. My foot got heavy. Up ahead was a spot in the road. It was a squirrel. I accelerated, but the squirrel did not. It was only a squirrel standing in the road. I was late. The stupid squirrel was too dumb to get out of the road. I got closer and closer. The squirrel had to die. At the last minute I couldn't do it. I stood on the breaks and decelerated from seriously speeding to almost zero before the darn little rodent scampered off the road.

As I sped up, I passed an old barn. On the other side was a police car. The officer was leaning forward tapping his radar machine. I sent a mental thank you to the squirrel. That would have been a very expensive ticket.

King Pig

Mail carriers see the dogs on our routes more often than we see their owners. Customers go about their lives but the dogs stay home to guard the house. Over the years, I have become good at judging dogs and their temperament. Is it nice? Will it bite or jump? Will the dog eat (or pee on) the parcel if I leave it? This is important information for my job.

Most customers have one or maybe two dogs. One of my customers had a herd of dogs. Not a pack. A pack is eight or nine. This customer had more than thirty. I don't know exactly because they wouldn't be still long enough to count. I tried. I have never seen that many dogs in one place outside of an animal shelter or a dog show. There were little dogs and big dogs, and even bigger dogs. When I drove up to the house the first time, they made an awful noise.

None of the dogs were aggressive so I looked down to gather the customer's mail and the parcel I was delivering. When the barking stopped abruptly, I looked up and there was not a dog in sight. They had disappeared. The whole herd of them. Then I saw the *pig*. A really, really big pig. It probably weighed more than three hundred pounds.

The pig slowly ambled up to my truck. I looked at it, and it looked at me. I wasn't afraid of the big herd of friendly dogs. But I was afraid of what scared a herd of dogs. I stayed in my truck.

THE LAUGHING POSTMAN

Part Six. Saving Lives

Gift Sister

One of my favorite families on my route lived on a lake. They had three children under five, and she watched her sister's three during the day. As fate would have it, they were all boys, but for one girl just under a year old. They received a lot of parcels. I would pull up to the back door and blow the horn.

Usually the mom would come out to the truck to get her mail and parcels. On this day, when the door opened the baby girl crawled out. And the door shut. The baby girl headed as fast as she could crawl toward the lake. I had mail on my lap, and threw it aside to scramble out of my truck. I reached her only a few feet from the water, and she giggled at my out-of-breath self.

Back at the door I rang the bell. Nothing. I knocked... after a moment a little voice replied... "Go away."

"I'm the mail lady" I answered, "I've got your little sister."

"We don't want her, you can have her!" multiple little voices said. I looked at the baby girl, she giggled at me. I rang the bell again. And again. When the door opened, it was a very wet, very irritated towel-wrapped mom. Her irritation changed to shock when she saw her daughter in my arms.

The door had been cleverly locked on the inside by multiple childproof latches. But five genius little boys with chairs, pillows, fly swatters and a butter knife had undone the locks in less time than a mom could take a shower.

It was luck that I happened by then.

Close Call

One of my favorite things to deliver on my mail route is photos. One day I had a COD parcel for a young mother. She had been waiting for me and met me at my truck. As she paid for the parcel and signed the paperwork, I saw her toddler crawl out the door. He negotiated his way down the steps by crawling backwards. Too cute.

The mom opened the photos and we admired them. She thanked me and headed toward the house. I asked her to find the baby before I backed out of the driveway. She said he was in the house asleep.

I reached over and turned off my truck. I wasn't moving until he was located. Mom started looking and calling. When she walked behind my truck I heard her gasp. The baby was sitting on my bumper.

After I left, I thought about what might have happened... then pulled over and threw up.

Life-saving Delays

Whenever I transferred to a new route, I had to learn a whole new set of customers and their particulars. Who was supposed to get mail at that address and who wasn't? Back door or front door? Good dog or bad dog? OK to leave parcels or not? Getting accustomed to a new set of potholes and mailboxes. And customers would want to get to know me.

The younger folks would want to know how long I had worked for the postal service or how I managed to drive from the passenger seat. Older customers also wanted to know how long I had been at the post office. And then they wanted to know to whom I was related. I found that, after a while, I just needed to find that connection as quickly as possible or be late on my route.

I was almost at the end of my new route and had

a parcel for an elderly lady. She was sitting on her porch as I dismounted to deliver the parcel. Of course I had to sit awhile. What was my name, who are my people, where did they originally come from, what church do I go to, am I married, who are his people, and where does he work. And so on... I was late but I also wanted to make a good impression on my new customers, so I answered her questions to her satisfaction. This put me several minutes later than I would have been.

On my way back to the post office I had to wait for a big accident. It had just happened and the ambulances were loudly announcing their approach. I realized that, except for my conversation with my new customer, I would have been on exactly that part of the road when the accident happened.

No Good Deed

Mrs. E was waiting on the other side of the road as I served her mailbox. We waived as I pulled away. I served two more boxes before I checked my rear view mirror. Mrs. E was lying in the road. I ran back to her and we could both hear a car coming around the curve. She begged me to help her out of the road. By my pulling under her arms and Mrs. E pushing with her legs, we got her to the side of the road.

The car came speeding around the curve and missed us by only a couple of feet. I'll never forget the look on the driver's face as he saw us. His eyes widened, and his face whitened. I knew that driver. Tom was also a customer, a young man with a young wife and a baby. He pulled over and came back to help. Tom was shaken by the chance he could have run over Mrs. E.

Tom and I got Mrs. E to her home and settled in

a chair. He made an ice pack and I got wet towels to help with the scrapes and cuts from the road. Mrs. E was more worried about leaving her stove on than the wounds. She thanked us profusely and wouldn't let us call anyone for her. Her daughter was on her way for lunch, she said, and sent us away. I felt good about helping Mrs. E.

A couple of weeks later, Mrs. E's daughter called me at the post office. When she introduced herself I expected gratitude. Instead she informed me that by moving Mrs. E I had broken her hip! The daughter told me that she was suing me, the post office and the horse I rode in on. I never heard from her again. No good deed...

Part Seven. And Everything Else

Body Parts

It was the busiest time of year for the post office, Christmas. We were understaffed and overworked. I was so tired and every muscle in my body hurt. So when I got a sharp pain in my side I thought it was just another ache. It persisted, though, so I went to the doctor.

During my exam my doctor noticed how worn down I was. "Take some time off," he said. I laughed. "The only way I can get time off at Christmas is if I die or have a body part removed," I told him.

It was his turn to laugh. "I can help you with that second part," he said. "You need an emergency cholecystectomy."

And that's how I got time off during Christmas—I had my gallbladder removed.

Radio Complaints

As a rural mail carrier, I am in my truck for six to nine hours a day, including route time and getting to and from work. It can get lonely and I depend on my radio a great deal. I listen to country, contemporary Christian, and rock music. I really like news and talk radio, too, and sometimes I get books on CD.

Because my right window is down while I'm driving, I play my radio loud—maybe a little too loud. Music can have bad words, talk radio is controversial, and my choice of books (romance) can have its own embarrassing bits.

The only complaint, however, that has ever been called in on me because of my loud radio choice was when I was playing the K-LOVE station. Christian radio.

Shade

Some of the irritating aspects of delivering mail are the scratches and dings we pick up using personal vehicles or postal trucks. The worst offender is a mailbox door that won't stay shut. They fall open just as I pull away. Bushes and trees are next on the list.

When a small oak tree growing between two mailboxes started getting big enough to scratch my truck, I asked the owner to cut it down. He didn't. Hearing that screeeetch as I pulled away drove me crazy, so one day I reached out and just broke off the offending branches. The owner didn't complain so as the tree grew I broke off more branches. Then I forgot about it.

Periodically I have to pull more mail from the back of my truck to the front. An idling truck is an overheating truck, so during the hottest part of the summer I plan my "reloads" for dismounts or shaded spots. I was sitting at one of my favorite shady places, organizing the mail for the next section of my route when I realized this was the tree that I had pruned so many years ago.

I leaned out and looked up. The canopy of the oak tree was beautiful, the shade a welcome respite from the summer sun, and I am very thankful the owner didn't cut it down those many, many years before.

4H and the Food Drive

Every May, the U.S. Postal Service holds its nationwide annual food drive. While it's a wonderful cause, loading, unloading and transferring the food to its donation truck is clearly a great deal of work for participating mail carriers.

In my off time, I am a 4H leader. With community service such a vital part of 4H, it seemed only natural to include my 4H club in the food drive. For the past five years, various club leaders have joined the cause.

Leaders drive and members jump from the vehicles to collect the food, load it in their vans or trucks, and return to the post office with full loads... only to unload and deposit them into assorted donation trucks.

Imagine my surprise when one of the other leaders was late returning. This was my most reliable volunteer, and our oldest group of 4Hers. They had the system down pat. When my cell phone rang showing her number on the ID, my first thought was to panic. When she handed her phone to one of the police officers surrounding her van, she wasn't laughing.

One of the neighborhood homeowners had seen the volunteers collecting food and assumed they were stealing. After more than forty years of volunteering and community service, her only response was... it took the U.S. Post Office food drive to make her a criminal.

Old Houses

I've noticed over the years that old houses hold up better than newer ones. When I say "old," I'm talking over a hundred years. A vacant new house starts to fall apart in a couple of years. The roof leaks and sags, mold grows, and trees crack the driveways and carports. Really old houses just get a little grayer and the paint peels. The tin roof rusts, but does not leak. No water damage, no mold. The trees are already bigger than the house.

Newer vacant houses look pitiful, while vacant old houses look sad.

An old house on my route had been vacant for years. Every spring the daffodils would bloom in smaller numbers in the untended flowerbeds. The estate was finally settled and the house was put up for sale. The old house was in good shape for a house from the pre-electric era. When the bulldozer unloaded, I was disappointed. Realistically, I understood that the land was more valuable than the house. But still.

To my delight, a crew carefully dismantled the house, board by numbered board. The crew boss told me they would be moving the house to a Heritage Village in Alabama, where it would be reconstructed. This was in the fall.

After the house was moved, the land was bulldozed and flattened. The next spring the daffodils exploded in righteous color. The bulldozer must have spread the bulbs. It was a joy to see.

Mailman Legend #1

In every profession there is someone extraordinary, someone who is a legend in the field. In my office that person is Mr. M. His motto is that no matter what, the mail has to be delivered and the route must be finished each and every day. Mr. M was most famous for delivering the mail after the transmission on his car messed up. The only gear that worked was reverse.

Yes, he finished his route... in reverse.

Mailman Legend #2

Once a year, our supervisors ride our routes with us. The reasons for this are to count the mailboxes and to observe our work. We think it's just to annoy us. Mr. M hated driving with the supervisors. So one year he arranged to use his son's vehicle—a hot rod. The supervisor had to sit in the cramped jump seat with his knees up to his chin. The funny part was that Mr. M. had several lake spillways on his route. And yes, Mr. M. ramped the spillways.

I'm told that he got good air and the supervisors never rode with him again.

Allergic Reaction

Bees are like dogs to mail carriers. It's not the big dogs that concern us; it's the killer Chihuahuas. Big wasps are like Rottweilers—slow to anger, threatening but open to apologies. Honeybees are like hound dogs—don't kick or squash them and they will leave you alone. And Guinea wasps are the Chihuahuas of the bee world... they want to kill you.

Guinea wasps can build a nest in a mailbox in less than twenty-four hours. Really. Monday I deliver mail to a wasp-free box. Tuesday I reach in to get the outgoing mail and get popped three times by the wasps before I even know they are there. Fortunately, I'm not allergic to bees or wasps.

By the time I returned to the post office my hand was itching and the little stings had become little bumps. No big deal. My supervisor thought otherwise and insisted I apply the bee anti-venom from the First Aid cabinet. By the time I got home my hand had swollen to twice its normal size.

I'm not allergic to bees. But I am very allergic to the bee anti-venom. Go figure.

Peeves

Garbage cans! Stinky smelly icky garbage cans blocking mailboxes!

Why do dogs have to take dumps in front of the mailbox? Right where the front wheel can't help but run over it. I probably look funny zigzagging for mud puddles to wash the poop off the tires.

I'm glad it's your child's birthday. But do you have to tie the mailbox door shut with the balloon strings?

Please don't put the mailbox flag up if you don't have outgoing mail. If you don't have any incoming mail I get to skip your box. My brake shoes thank you.

I am only human. I work thousands of pieces of mail a day. Please don't write on mail that is not yours, just put it back in the box. My substitute is more human and less experienced than I am. Don't throw rocks.

If your dog has teeth, yes it can too bite.

Staples in mail can cause injury to the mail carrier. Bleeding on the mail is against postal policy.

A big fat lipstick smeared kiss on a letter is icky— very, very icky.

Forty-six pennies for a stamp is o.k. Forty-six pennies loose in a mailbox is not o.k. Please, please, containerize your money.

Dropping Babies

Some people let plants, usually climbing varieties, grow on their mailboxes. It can be very pretty and I don't mind as long as there are no poison ivy or briers. Sometimes it can turn into a jungle that scratches my truck.

I was eight-and-a-half months pregnant with my third child. Having the mailbox engulfed in so much beautiful variegated ivy made it hard to open the box. As I started to open the box a large green snake poked his head out of the ivy. From my position the snake was eye level and only inches away. I decided to take the mail to the door.

When the lady answered the door, I told her about the snake. I told her that unless she wanted me to drop my baby in her yard, she needed to trim the mailbox.

The next day, the ivy had been trimmed—all the way to the ground.

Postal Pessimist vs. Optimist

Pessimist: Damn, it's raining.

Optimist: Mr. G's vegetable garden needed this!

Pessimist: It's too hot/cold.

Optimist: It's a beautiful day!

Pessimist: Damn box holders.

Optimist: Mrs. S can plan her grocery shopping!

Pessimist: Too many parcels.

Optimist: Happy, happy customers today!

Pessimist: Too much mail.

Optimist: Job security!

Pessimist: Stupid safety/service talk...

Optimist: Wow, I needed to know that!

Pessimist: Yea it's payday!

Optimist: Yea it's payday!

VOLUME TWO. THE LAUGHING

POSTMAN DELIVERS

THE LAUGHING POSTMAN

Part One. Dogs

Wrangling Puppies

One very hot summer, I had a special delivery for a customer at the end of a long, winding driveway. The customer wasn't home but I was greeted by three grown Jack Russell terriers and a gaggle of puppies. Sixteen puppies. Ask me how I know!

When I parked my truck, the adult dogs ran up to greet me as usual. We were friends of long standing. And of course the puppies followed. I congratulated the adult on her fine progeny while the puppies leaped and tumbled over each other. And in typical puppy style, they grew tired and plopped down for naps. Under my truck!

I got out of my truck and herded the puppies back towards the house. Now this was a fine new game for them. As soon as I got back into the truck, they piled under it again.

I saw a large cage on the porch and started the

task of capturing puppies and containerizing them. After half a dozen wiggling puppies were successfully safe in the pen, the others caught on and the task got harder. I had to crawl under my truck to get the last three. Sixteen puppies!

At the end of the long driveway, I wiped sweat from my face and took a deep drink of cold water. I realized if I were hot and thirsty, the penned puppies would be also. Not knowing when the owners would come home, I went back up the long driveway to find a bowl and a water faucet. Of course some puppies escaped during this procedure and had to be recaptured.

I had spent over thirty minutes at one of my 672 stops. I accounted for the time to my supervisor as "puppy wrangling."

Spinning Dog

I had a very large German shepherd on my route. He would bark and growl and otherwise make such a fuss that I didn't get out at that address. He would also chase cars.

One of my personal nightmares is the possibility of running over someone's beloved pet. I would pay close attention to the dogs on my route that were most likely to run in the road. This shepherd was different. Most dogs would run alongside my car until I got out of their territory. This one would wait until I pulled away from the mailbox and then start spinning in circles as I drove by. Weird.

One day, I started to leave the mailbox when I noticed the large dog was very close to my car. I braked but the spinning had already started. About four spins in the dizzy dog slammed into my motionless car. He knocked himself silly and staggered away.

The owner of the dog, a young man, was in the yard. He walked over to the stunned dog and just shook his head.

"I didn't hit him," I explained. The man just laughed.

The man told me the dog had spent most of his life and an animal shelter before the family had adopted him. The dog had grown up in a small pen and when he got excited he would spin in circles.

I guess chasing the mail lady was exciting.

The Jekyll and Hyde Dog

Ozzie was a Weimaraner dog. I first met him as a puppy and he was beautiful. He had silver-grey fur and blue eyes. He grew up to be one of the gentlest, sweetest dogs on my route. When I would drive up he would bound up to the truck with his whole body wagging.

I had a parcel for Ozzie's house and I was looking forward to seeing him. When I drove up to the house I noticed there were extra cars. I dismounted and had started around the truck when Ozzie came from the house. He was growling and foaming at the mouth! The hair on his back was sticking up like bristles and he lunged at me like he was attacking. I was shocked. I backed up to the truck, preparing to hold him off with the parcel while I got back in.

Ozzie's owner ran up and grabbed his collar, apologizing. I asked her if he was sick, as I was

thinking that he must have rabies to act that way.
Just then, two small children came out of the house.
Ozzie became even more aggressive. His owner
explained that when the grandkids were visiting,
Ozzie became extremely protective.

Sure enough, the next time I had a parcel for that
address, Ozzie was his usual sweet self. No children:
Dr. Jekyll; children: Mr. Hyde.

Shredded Mail

Occasionally, mail gets damaged. Sometimes a parcel gets dented or a letter gets crumbled or torn in the machines. The carriers usually get these as the final step in a process but of course we get all the blame.

I take extra care with the mail I deliver. My creed is biblical: treat the mail as I would want my personal mail treated. Do-not-bends, fragile parcels and medicines are handled with care. My main problem is keeping the mail dry when it is storming. I will confess that on one occasion I purposely and with malice shredded a customer's magazine.

It happened like this. Dogs can be a problem. Usually the problem occurs when we are outside the vehicle. Sometimes the dang dog bites a hole in a tire when we are in the vehicle. I had a bad dog, a bulldog, who liked to hide by his mailbox and ambush me. He would lunge out of the bushes and scare me. The first time this happened, I jerked my hand back into the car so fast I let go of the mail and it flew across the car. Luckily the opposite window was closed.

The day I shredded the mail, the bulldog didn't stop his lunge when I pulled my arm back into the window. He kept coming. And coming. Until the large, angry, toothy dog was through the window and into the car and inches from my face. Desperate, I used the handful of mail I was about to put in his owner's mailbox to push the dog back out of my car.

And while the dog lay on the ground, I calmly, without guilt, placed the shredded mail in the mailbox.

Wash Them There Apples

This happened to a coworker. He had a crate of apples to deliver on his route. Crates for fruit have holes to allow circulation to keep the fruit from rotting. He didn't know about the German shepherd in residence. About half way to the porch with the heavy parcel, my coworker was charged by the very large, very angry dog. Understand that this coworker is a large man. He did what any large man would do: he dropped the crate and ran.

Back in the safety of his truck, he looked for the dog. The shepherd had stopped at the sacrificial parcel and was doing what large male dogs do to mark their territory. My coworker commented that he hoped the customer washed the apples before eating them.

Jumping Jack

One of the funny but also endearing facts about small breed dogs is that they don't recognize that they are not large. Take miniature pinschers. Please. They are small dogs with a giant attitude. I fear them second only to Chihuahuas. Truly, I would rather deal with a German shepherd or a Rottweiler than a small dog.

Jack was a seven-year-old miniature pinscher on my mail route. He lived with the manager of a trailer park and spent his days on demolition. He should have been named Shredder. Tiny pieces of dog toys, kid toys, yard ornaments and tennis balls covered the property like graffiti. He was determined to add my arm to his collection.

There were seven mailboxes in a row. Jack considered it his ultimate goal in life to rip my arm off as I served those mailboxes. Never mind that he was a small dog and I was in a truck. He believed he could leap five feet in the air at just the right time and shred my arm. And I believed he could, too.

This is how I accomplished my goal of delivering the mail while preventing Jack from his goal of sinking teeth into my flesh. I would reach out, open the mailbox, and jerk my arm back in the truck. Jack would jump up. When he was on the way down, I would put the mail in the box and jerk my arm back into the truck as he jumped again. One more trip to the box to close the lid, one more jumping Jack. If a mailbox had outgoing mail, I would add two more steps to this procedure—one to put the flag down and one to get the mail out.

Times seven.

Saved by the Chain

I was in a new delivery area and was learning where to leave the parcels. The front door on a particular address didn't look like it had been used in a while, so I started around the house towards the back door. I heard a low-throated growl and looked up to see a huge German shepherd running towards me.

The dog was in a full out charge for me and I froze. Post office training says to never turn your back on an angry dog but I didn't even have time for that. I put the parcel in front of my face and closed my eyes just as the dog launched. My last thought was, *I'm gonna die!*

I heard a "thunk" and then nothing. Opening my eyes, I stared at the killer dog at my feet. He had hit the end of his chain two feet in front of me.

Saved by the chain.

Magic Words

I was very young when I started working for the post office. For many years I was the youngest in the rural carrier craft and the old-timers called me "baby duck" and "the apprentice." They would give me advice and tell me tall tales.

One carrier who was nearing retirement said he had the secret to controlling vicious dogs. It was two magic words. The words, this wizard of a mailman explained, had to be spoken in just the right way to be effective. He gifted these words to me and had me practice until I had the delivery of the words perfect.

Years later, these words saved me from a vicious dog. I was on a new route and was taking a parcel to the door when a large, angry dog attacked. I didn't have time to run so I said the magic words.

The dog was about to leap when I shouted with a firm, disapproving voice, "BAD DOG!"

The dog tucked his tail, hung his head and slunk away.

Shocking!

One of the small nuisances of being a mail carrier is static charge buildup. On a dry, windy day, I can build up quite a charge. When I get out of the truck and touch the door, I get zapped. After a few pops you learn to ground yourself by holding on to the door before you step out.

This way, the charge goes in the ground.

Another, not so small, nuisance is bad dogs. One of my customers has a very nice shepherd. She is a sweetie. One bright, dry, windy day, I got out of my truck to deliver a parcel at her house. She trots up, wagging her body, as happy to see me as I am to see her. Problem was she had company. A not-so-nice bulldog from the next block was visiting.

I saw the moment he decided that his girlfriend's casa was his casa. He started growling and I started backing up. I held my hand out with my fingers curled to let him sniff while I eased toward my truck. He sniffed and the static charge I'd built up left my knuckle and shot up his nose. I actually saw the spark.

He yelped and took off for home.

Dog Eats Shoe

When I first started as a mail carrier, I didn't know that it was a good thing to leave the vehicle door open when taking mail up to a residence. One of the more experienced carriers may have warned me but, then again, maybe not.

It was a beautiful day as I dismounted my car and headed up to door to deliver a signature-required letter. Then the bulldog crawled from under the truck and came for me. I sprinted back to my small car as fast as I could. The dog was close on my heels and I didn't have time to open the door so I just dove in through the window.

The entire time it took me to get right side up the dog was chewing on my shoe. He ripped the shoelace and tore the sock but did not break my skin. I finally got in the seat properly and rolled up the window. My elbow was banged and my face bruised from the console but that wasn't the worst of it.

The customer was standing in the yard laughing at me. Now I always leave the truck door open when I go up to a house.

Unauthorized Passengers

When mail carriers get out of their vehicles, they leave the door open. We might dismount up to a hundred times a day and it saves time. Also we might need to get back in the vehicle very quickly.

I had left the door open at the home of one of my favorite customers when their little Yorkie dog decided she wanted to go with me. When I tried to grab her, she jumped to the back seat. When I reached in the back seat, she jumped to the front. It took her owner and me to capture her. The cute little dog and her owner were laughing at me. I thought it was funny, too.

One of my coworkers had a different experience. She had a small, two-door car and she was pretty small herself. On a stormy cold day she delivered a parcel to the door and returned to find a passenger sitting on the mail. It was a sheepdog. He was a very large, very friendly, very wet and muddy sheepdog.

He probably weighed more than she did. And he had no interest whatsoever in vacating the warm, dry car. She tried pulling him out but he braced himself and did not budge. Meanwhile the rain was pouring down. She finally managed to evict him by getting in the opposite side and pushing him out with her feet and legs.

If any of her customers wondered about the muddy paw prints, they never called it in.

Part Two. Love My Customers

Good Groceries

One hot summer day, I was delivering in an older neighborhood when a small public bus blocking the mailboxes delayed me. I was irritated at the delay until I saw Mrs. C getting out with her hands full with grocery bags. The bus drove off, leaving the elderly lady by the curb with her bags.

Of course I got out and helped her move the bags to her porch. She was thankful and insisted on giving me a glass of sweet iced tea. She explained that she bought groceries every first and third Tuesday.

I would watch for the bus on those days and time my delivery so that I could help her with the groceries. Every time the proud lady would thank me with homemade goodies: iced drinks on hot days, homemade cookies in the fall, and hearty soups from the Crockpot in the cold winter.

She was a great cook and those were some good groceries.

My Hero

I have always tried to be the best mail carrier I can be. I've treated the mail for my customers as I would want my mail treated. I have gone the extra mile, literally and figuratively. And my customers have done the same for me. I have received warm muffins on cold days, ice water on hot days and kind notes on days I was unhappy.

My oldest daughter was in the National Guard and served in the Gulf War. She was flying home for leave midway through her tour and I was so very excited to see her. Her plane wasn't due in until late so I chose to work that day. And Murphy struck.

First, the truck that brought my office the mail broke down and was late. I had an extra heavy parcel count. And then I had a flat tire and my jack broke. I was going to be late to pick up my baby from the airport. I cried.

One of my customers saw my predicament and came to the rescue. He had a huge jack and made short work of changing my tire. When I told him my soldier girl was coming home he said that she was a hero for serving her country. I agreed.

I told him that, for helping me, HE was my hero.

Penny Stamps

I know that some of my older customers are on fixed incomes—that they sometimes make hard choices between medicines and food, necessities and luxuries.

When the price of fuel skyrockets, the postal service is forced to raise prices to compensate. Our business *is* transportation of the mail. Our competitors can change their prices at their convenience but we have to get permission from Congress. And Congress only lets us raise prices in penny increments.

So, for a while, every couple of months the price of a stamp would go up one cent. Explaining this to my customers took hours on my route. I finally decided to just buy ten dollars' worth of penny stamps and put them on myself. It saved time and I felt bad for my fixed income customers.

I got a very long, very irate letter from one of those customers. She wanted to know what happened to her under-stamped mail. Did it go to a dead letter office, or did the addressed person have to pay for it?

I explained that I had put the extra stamps on her mail to save time. This only made her angrier. She wasn't a "charity case," she informed me hotly. She figured up every increase in postage and every letter she had mailed and paid me back.

In pennies. One hundred and thirty-two pennies.

Alzheimer's

Years ago, I had a customer who called in to complain that I had placed someone else's mail in his box and gave his mail to the neighbor. I didn't think I had done so, but it was an overburdened route, over ten hours a day, and I am only human. So for the next several days I paid particular attention to that address and was sure I made no mistakes. But the man called in again and again.

My supervisor gave me an official discussion about my mistakes and threatened suspension. I told him to ride the route with me and he could watch me deliver the mail to that customer. He agreed and double-checked the mail before I put it in the box. When we returned to the post office, there was a message from the customer that I had messed up again.

My supervisor called the man back, ready to

defend me, but the man's wife answered instead. She thought it was funny. That mistake, she explained, had happened years before. Her husband had Alzheimer's and was fixated on the mail. She stopped laughing when my boss told her I had almost been fired. She apologized and, from then on, we ignored all complaints from that address.

Divorce!

I had a certified letter for a customer. Her car was in the driveway so I knew she was home. As I walked by her car, I saw something strange wedged by her back tire. It was the bottom half of a broken beer bottle with jagged pieces pointed up.

If my customer had backed up she would have ruined the tire. I went on to the house and got her signature for the letter. I asked her to come see what I had found. She wasn't surprised and thanked me for noticing.

I asked who would do that. She shrugged and said two words: "Bad divorce."

Stamp Money

Rural letter carriers take pride in full postal services. When "rural free mail delivery" became widespread in the early 1900s, the rural carrier was a post office on wheels. If a customer lived on a rural postal route they had no reason to travel to a post office. The carrier could handle almost everything.

One of these services is the purchase of stamps. The post office provides special brightly colored stamp order envelopes for that purpose but often a customer will use other envelopes or containers for their stamp money. Sometimes they just put the money loose in the mailbox.

So it wasn't unusual to stop at a mailbox with the flag up and find a plain white envelope with the word "STAMPS" written on it. What was unusual was the amount of money. Three hundred and twenty-seven dollars. My first thought was I didn't carry that many stamps with me. At the time, a book of twenty stamps cost $5.00. Usually my stamp volume for a day was about three books and another 15 individual stamps. When I sold more than I carried with me, I filled the order that afternoon and delivered the next day.

Three hundred and twenty-seven dollars was a lot of stamps. This address was a retired couple. They didn't have a business or tons of correspondence. In fact they usually bought their stamps one dollar's worth at a time. So I went up to the house to ask.

As I approached the door I heard yelling and the sounds of demolition. I knocked. Waited. Knocked again. Silence, then the door opened and the very haggard elderly man stood there. Behind him the living room looked like a tornado had landed. The couch cushions were on the floor, papers scattered every which way. I showed the man the envelope but before I could speak he reached out, grabbed it and slammed the door in my face.

I heard him yell, "I found it!" I guessed that

answered that.

When I was half way to my car, the door reopened and my customer called me back. He explained that the money was for monthly bills and he and his wife had been frantically searching for it. I guess they would have been surprised to find 1,308 stamps in their mailbox the next day.

Black Eyes and Poker Faces

The postal service offers free forwarding for first- and second-class mail when customers change their addresses. Businesses can purchase the new address for a small fee by simply requesting this in writing.

This can be a problem in certain situations.

I cannot lie. I stutter and stammer and can't make eye contact. While this put me at a disadvantage as a child, I have a great reputation. On the other hand, I have a really good poker face. As long as I don't have to verbally lie, I can refrain from telling all truths—and keep a straight face.

I had a young couple in an upscale neighborhood on my mail route. They had it all—a new house and cars, landscaped, manicured lawn and designer dogs. I envied them. Until the day the young wife intercepted me a block from her home.

She had two black eyes, a huge multicolored

bruise on her jaw, a taped swollen nose and stitches over one eyebrow. She was frightened and asked me for a change of address card. I gave her one but explained how easy it was for someone to get that new address. I told her I would talk to my postmaster.

The solution was we would not put the change of address into the system. I would personally write her new address on each piece of mail.

The next day the husband waited for me by their mailbox. He said he and his wife had a small disagreement and he just wanted to apologize. Did I know where she went? I looked at the scabs on his knuckles and then straight into his sorry-ass eyes.

"Nope," I told him. "We have no forwarding on file."

Don't Mess with the Mail Lady!

I had transferred to a new route and was just getting comfortable with the territory and learning the details of each address. Because I was new, I was running later in the day than the previous carrier. Some customers would meet me at their box to introduce themselves and to chat. This of course made me even later although I was glad to put a face with the address.

I was almost finished with the route when I saw a customer waiting. He was not interested in being friendly but was upset about not receiving his check. He didn't have any mail that day but refused to believe me. Cursing, he reached in to grab the incoming mail on my dash that I picked up from customers. I told him to get out and again that he had no mail for that day. I was becoming concerned. This was BC (before cell phones). My only option was to push him out and drive away, possibly injuring the man.

From the other side of my car I heard a deep voice ask, "What you doin' man?"

The first man leaned out of my car and straightened up. "The b# has my check and won't give it to me," he screamed.

The other man standing by my car was very tall and I couldn't see his face. "You don't get a check idiot. Are you stupid? Nobody messes with the mail lady!"

The shorter man looked at the other man over the top of my car, turned and ran away.

My rescuer leaned way down to look at me with a kind face. "Don't worry 'bout him, Mail Lady, me and him will have a little talk later."

I whispered, a little shook up, "I really don't have his check today."

"'Course not," the big man smiled. "That fool don't get a check. It goes straight in the bank. He just forgets is all."

Small Customers

Many years ago, I was met at a mailbox by a young girl holding the ugliest doll I had ever seen. The child was frowning.

"You!" she accused, "You folded and creased my baby's birth certificate!"

She went on to tell me that she had planned to frame the certificate and that the collectability of her baby was lessened by my negligence. She had more coming and asked that I please be considerate and not destroy them.

My coworkers educated me about Cabbage Patch dolls. I watched for the certificates. When they came, they were in an oversized envelope, bulk rate with no special handling instructions. No "Do Not Bend" notice. I hadn't really done anything wrong.

I remembered the little girl's disappointed face. I didn't want to be the cause of her bad experience with the United States Postal Service. I treated her mail as fragile. Later I added mail from dog and horse registries to that category even though they had no special handling indicated.

The girl's family moved away soon after that. She received more birth certificates. They were not first class mail and could not be forwarded. I hand-wrote her new address and "Do Not Bend." I paid the postage.

That happened more than twenty-five years ago. My motto for treating the mail became do unto it as that little girl would want done.

United States Postal *Service*!

THE LAUGHING POSTMAN

Part Three. Critters

His Damn Fish!

The hardest thing about learning a new mail route is learning all the names that belong to each address. Most people don't know that, because of the Privacy Act, the postal service purges forwarding information after 18 months. Mail carriers are required to deliver all mail as addressed unless we have information in writing otherwise or "personal knowledge."

Sometimes that personal knowledge is hard won. My third day on a new route I opened a mailbox to find the letter I had left the day before.

Written on it in bright red ink were the words: G. BIRD DOES NOT LIVE HERE ANYMORE! HIS DAD DOES NOT LIVE HERE ANYMORE! HIS CAT DOESN'T LIVE HERE AND HIS DAMN FISH DOESN'T LIVE HERE! I DON'T KNOW WHERE THE HELL HE IS. OK?

For the Birds

Birds and mailboxes go together like peas and carrots. Most of the year the birds use the outside of the box as a resting perch and a latrine. In the spring, however, mailboxes become a tempting dry place to build a nest. Usually these are mailboxes without a lid or with one that doesn't fit well. An energetic and desperate mother-to-be can build a nest and lay eggs between the Saturday mail delivery and Monday.

Some customers, when faced with a bird nest in their box, will discourage the little moms by removing the nest. Most people will just abide for the few weeks it takes for the babies to grow and fly away. I'm careful when I put the mail in and the customers are careful when they take the mail out.

The problem I've had with birds in the mailbox is that I forget. I drive up to the box with mail in hand, and letters going in meet a bird coming out.

Sometimes the bird ends up in the vehicle and the mail on the ground. I've actually given myself whiplash when a bird explodes out of a box into my face.

The most startling episode I've had with birds didn't involve a mailbox. I had a long stretch of road with open fields on either side and no mail stops in sight. Speeding along with my window down, I noticed a flock of black birds approaching. I had just enough time to think, *Those birds are flying a little low*, when they ducked under the power line and flew across the road. Like the Titanic, the twain met. Most of the birds corrected and didn't hit my truck. Two large birds flew in the window.

I was traveling 55 miles an hour. Not sure how fast the birds were going. A mass of feathers passed my face and then went splat against the back seat. I managed to not crash my truck and I pulled over. Silence in the back seat. Expecting dead birds, I got out and opened the back door. Stunned by living birds eyeing me in fear. With a little encouragement

I got the birds out of my truck with only some feathers and poop for souvenirs.

Scary Bugs

Mailboxes attract bugs. Maybe it's the color of the box, or the mostly dry interiors.

I've encountered: red wasps, Guinea wasps, honeybees, dirt dabbers, carpenter bees, black widow spiders, brown widow spiders, wolf spiders, huge garden spiders (also known as banana spiders), the southern house spider, grass spiders, false black widows, brown recluse, praying mantises, cockroaches, ladybugs, assassin bugs, longhorn beetles, stink bugs, box elder bugs, carpenter ants, fire ants, earwigs, leaf-footed bugs, katydids, giant mayflies, walking sticks, June beetles, moths, granddaddy longlegs, cicadas, wheel bugs, and pine beetles. And I'm able to identify all these because my youngest child was an avid bug collector in 4H. She would want me to tell you that the list includes not just insects but Arachnidan and true bugs.

After many days of drenching rain, fire ants will move their entire nest into a mailbox. I've opened the lid of a box and come face to squirming ickyness with a mass of ants and eggs.

Ladybugs also like to hibernate in mailboxes. One winter I had three boxes full of ladybugs. Two owners removed theirs but one asked me to be "gentle" and we carefully placed the mail in and out for weeks.

This is my weirdest encounter: A nest of harvestmen (also known as granddaddy longlegs) hatched on the lid of one of my mailboxes. There were literally hundreds of the tiny guys. Over the next days they grew. And grew. I could open the lid at first but when they got bigger they moved and shutting the lid would smash some. So I used my hand to push them away from the edge. The next day they would be back in the way. I did this for several days.

I would pull up to the box, gently herd the longlegs to the center, open the lid, put the mail in, close the lid and drive away. After several days of this I pulled up to the box and started to wave them away from the edge but, before I reached out, they moved as a group to the center. I stared for a moment, not sure what I had just witnessed. I put the lid down, mail in, and lid up. The critters all moved back in unison to the center of the lid. They did it again the next day. And every day after until one day they were all gone.

Peek-a-Boo

We in the South love our green lawns. Some people plant winter hardy rye grass so their yard is green all year round. This is a boost to the wildlife as it benefits rabbits, deer and even birds.

I had a parcel for a house at the end of a twisty, narrow driveway surrounded by bushes and thick oak trees. Nearer the house, the woods thinned and became younger oak trees. The customer had planted rye grass and the greenery was a welcome sight in the brown winter. And delicious to the three deer feeding in the yard. I stopped my truck to watch them. Two ran off when they saw me.

The third deer, the smallest, didn't run off. She walked behind a small oak tree and faced it so she couldn't see me. Every few seconds she would peek around the tree trunk to see if I was still there, then jerk her head back behind the tree. It was a small tree and in no way hid the deer.

I guess she thought that if she couldn't see, me I couldn't see her.

Spider Dance

As a new hire, I was told that there were three ways to get fired: losing the key that unlocks all the centralized freestanding dismounted mailboxes, having an accident while backing up, and not getting signatures for accountable mail.

The key is a big ole thing on a long chain. I ran the chain through my belt loop on my shorts so that I wouldn't forget to remove the key when I finished serving those boxes. The mailboxes were grouped in large metal rectangles with one large door in the back that I would open and then sort the mail into smaller slots for the individual customers. Customers often waited for their mail.

I had received a Walkman (yes, this dates me) as a present and would listen to music with earphones while I served the boxes. One day, several customers were standing around when I opened the door. An extremely large spider crawled out, bounced off my shirt, and ran down my shorts and then back up the shorts—all in a split second. I jumped backwards, ripping the chain from my shorts and hopped around like crazy trying to dislodge the spider without causing it to bite me.

After what seemed like a long time but was probably only a couple of seconds, the spider abandoned me for the safer world of the parking lot. As I was catching my breath, one of the watching customers asked, "Break dancing?"

"No," I replied, "Spider dance."

Part Four. Mail Carriers

Don't Eat the Fruitcake

When a carrier transfers from one route to another, he or she usually gives tips and help with the transition. Another way of passing information is what we call a route book. This short, hand-written notebook is filled with notes describing the driving directions, order of the mailboxes and current addressees. Being an aspiring writer, I also included in my route book past addressees, best place for parcels, bad dogs (highlighted in pink), day sleepers, and pretty much everything else I could think of.

It was with pride that I handed this postal version of the Great American Novel to the new carrier on the route. I heard nothing from my replacement carrier for days. The book must have been so good that I only got one question from the carrier.

She wanted to know why I had written and highlighted in yellow the words "Don't Eat the

Fruitcake" by one of the addresses. I explained that the customer gave me a fruitcake every Christmas— and that I had personally delivered a case of fruitcakes to that address in 1983. It was the *only* case of fruitcakes. *Ever.*

I told this story in 1991.

Stop Signs Are Not Optional

Sometimes being a mail carrier means breaking the law. Sort of. Unless we have a right-hand drive vehicle, most rural carriers sit in the middle or even in the passenger seat to drive. We use our left foot for the brake and accelerator and our left hand to drive. We use our right hand to deliver the mail. Also, it's not possible to wear the seat belt and deliver mail. The twisting, leaning, and turning causes the seat belt to get tighter and tighter.

My route included part of a four-lane highway. Sometimes crossing that traffic was a hassle. I had a left turn at the top of a hill and I could see the traffic lined up solid for miles. There was one break in the line of vehicles but to take advantage of it I would have to run a stop sign. Otherwise I would be sitting on that hill forever. I ran the stop sign.

I had stopped at my next mailbox when a

highway patrol car pulled in behind me with its lights flashing. I was guilty but I'm not above begging to get out of a ticket. As the officer ran my tags I practiced my plea. I had an Express that had to be delivered by 3 P.M. I had to meet the dispatch truck. (This is the truck that takes the outgoing mail I collect each day.)

The officer left his car and headed to my driver side door, flipping his ticket book open. "Stop signs are not optional," he said in a stern voice, looking up to the empty driver seat.

His eyes tracked to me in the passenger seat while I started to stammer my excuses. He said, with disgust, "You're a mail carrier!"

He ripped the ticket out of his book and crumpled it up. He went back to his car, turned off his lights and drove away.

Just in case, I don't run stop signs anymore. That's my story.

School Buses and Tractors

When my grandfather delivered the mail, the roads were mostly gravel and the houses were far apart. The mail routes could be over a hundred miles long with only two or three hundred deliveries. Modern routes are half the miles with three times the customers.

Gravel roads and the rainy season make for interesting driving. My grandfather told me how hard it was to pull on and off the road to serve the mailboxes. And when the shoulders of the road grew soft with lots of rain, it was easy to get stuck. He carried a shovel and a contraption called a come-a-long for getting unstuck. Even then, sometimes getting stuck in the mud meant waiting for someone to pull you out.

He was in a ditch one rainy day trying to find rocks or branches to put under a tire for traction when the school bus went by. The kids thought it was funny and of course the bus splashed more mud on him. He tried a while longer then decided he would have to walk to the nearest house for help. Remember, this was BC (before cell phones).

He was walking up the road when a farmer driving a tractor met him. The man came prepared with raincoats and chains for pulling my grandfather's truck out of the ditch. They took care of business and got the truck back on the road.

My grandfather asked the farmer how he knew he was stuck and needed help.

"School bus went by. You didn't," was all the man said.

My Customers

My day as a rural carrier starts in the post office by putting the mail in route order. The magazine-size mail is sorted to my route in tubs and the letter-size in trays.

As we work, we sometimes talk to the carrier next to us even though we can't see each other. I was telling my neighbor that I was glad a parcel had arrived for one of my customers who had been looking for it the day before.

A voice behind me interrupted, "Your customer? You don't own the customer. Those are post office customers." My supervisor had snuck up to listen to our conversation.

My boss had a sneer on his face. I picked up a letter at random from my case, glanced at it and held it out to the man. "What do you see?" I asked him.

He looked at the letter, confused. "I see 37 cents

and that and a lot more is my paycheck."

"I see Mrs. K. She buried her husband three months ago. This is a letter from her daughter. There are probably photos of the grandkids in this. Sometime today Mrs. K will go to her mailbox and see this letter. Maybe she will smile and for a little while not be as sad," I told him.

I picked up another letter. The boss laughed. "That's a bill. Nobody likes bills."

"Wrong," I said. "This customer has a home business. He puts ads in the newspaper and the phone is his contact. Today I will leave this phone bill and tomorrow he will mail his payment. And for another month his line of communication will be assured."

My supervisor just looked at me, a puzzled expression on his face. He didn't get it. I have 672 customers. United States Postal *Service*.

Changing Tires

As a rural letter carrier for the U. S. Postal Service, I use my personal vehicle to deliver the mail. I get compensated for this with a mileage allotment. Thirty-two years ago this allotment was enough to pay for gas, oil changes, brake maintenance, and tires. Today it is barely enough for the gas and oil. A bittersweet joke is that I have to have a truck to do the job, and that I have to have the job to pay for the truck!

Brake shoes and pads are an issue. I change my front brakes about every three months, back brakes every six months. And I get new rotors frequently. Some of the mechanically inclined carriers actually take brake parts on the route and change them when the first squeak happens.

Tires are also a financial issue. Tires wear out. Especially the tire that drops off the road into that little dip in front of your box. And before you complain, no—I don't spin out *on purpose*. It's just that getting back to the blacktop takes a little extra acceleration. Also, when the ground is wet, a layer of mud leaves with me every time, further deepening the spot.

Tires get holes. Nails, screws, wires from other shredded tires, sharp rocks, bolts, sticks, and bones have all been pulled from my flat tires. And once an arrowhead. No, you don't get to hear the joke the repairman told.

Usually I'm in the middle of nowhere when I get a flat. I changed my first flat the day I got my driver's license. It wasn't actually flat which, to my teenaged self, seemed a waste of time. Thanks, Dad. No really, thanks.

Most of the time a Good Samaritan would help me with flat tires. On one memorable occasion I was in a rapidly growing subdivision when I got a flat. I was eight months pregnant, struggling with a too-small jack as truckloads of construction workers passed me by. Some of them actually laughed. None stopped.

And what is it with those mini jacks? I hated them. I was on a route with warehouses when I noticed a low tire. Not wanting to fight with the baby jack I went in to ask if one of the owners of a large truck would let me borrow his real jack so I could change my tires. I wasn't asking him to change it for me but he offered to help.

Another time, I was waiting by my car with the spare tire out when a forklift came around the corner. The driver grinned and asked if I needed a lift!

That was the easiest tire I've ever changed.

Flags

The red flag on a mailbox is supposed to be used to indicate to the mailman that the customer has outgoing mail to be picked up. When it is up, we expect to remove the outgoing mail before we place today's mail in the box. We put the flag down so that the next time the customer has outgoing mail he or she can put it up again. If the flag is up and no mail is present we worry that the mail might have been stolen.

Usually it is just the customer using the flag to see if we have served their box that day. This is a pet peeve of mail carriers. If we don't have mail for that box but the flag is up, we have to stop and look. No mail means we could have skipped that box and saved time.

One of the old-timers at my office bragged that if the customer kept putting the flag up with no outgoing mail, he would write them a note asking them not to do that. If they continued, he would rip the flag off the box. We thought he was joking but when he retired the new carrier found the collection of mailbox flags in the back of his drawer.

One of my customers had no flag on her antique mailbox. She used a red scarf to indicate when she had outgoing mail. I would smile when I came around the curve and saw that scarf blowing in the wind. Her children recently replaced their mom's old mailbox with a shiny new one, complete with flag.

I miss that red waving scarf.

Ho, Ho, Ho!

Christmas is a difficult time for mail carriers. Rural carriers have a greatly increased workload without increased pay. This is because rural carrier's wages are salaried, based on an actual physical count of all the mail that a route gets during a two- or four-week time period, usually in what we carriers consider a "light" volume mail period.

Our contract allows overtime pay during a couple of weeks right before Christmas but the heavy mail volume actually starts before Thanksgiving. Management puts the pressure on when the overtime period begins. That pressure, plus the hectic time of year, and weather, and increased parcels, creates a stressful environment.

There are compensations. I personally like delivering parcels. Customers are happy to see the mail carrier with a parcel. Not so much when all I have is a handful of bills and advertisements. And sometimes I receive a "happy" in the mailbox. Recently I got a warm cranberry pecan muffin. Yummy. Even a nice note is greatly appreciated. And the Christmas decorations are beautiful.

Years ago, I worked in a neighborhood where all the residents decorated their front doors for the holidays. It became an adventure to walk up to a door and admire the creativity that went into the decorations. So it was with happy anticipation that I walked up to a door with a Santa Claus smiling down at me. I didn't expect anyone to answer the door (both cars were gone) so I rang the bell and admired the Santa. Then right by my ear a booming voice shouted "HO, HO, HO! MERRY CHRISTMAS!" Startled, I jumped three feet in the air and slung the fistful of mail at the Santa.

I am very glad that this happened years ago. Nowadays, I could expect to see myself on YouTube with the title "Mail Carrier Attacks Santa Claus."

Note to Self

Sadly, the post office has gotten a bad reputation for violence in the workplace. As a thirty-plus-year employee and a third-generation rural carrier, I have been in the trenches, so to speak. I'm glad that I never witnessed physical violence in the workplace. But I have witnessed and experienced physiological and emotional abuse.

Today I am happy to say that my work environment couldn't be better. My bosses are great people. Any issues that come up are handled with respect and understanding on both sides. I hear and read that this is not so in other offices and it brings back unpleasant memories.

I was hired during a period when rural carrier substitutes were not allowed to convert to full time or to join the union. We were jokingly referred to as scrubs. The pay was good, however: three times the minimum wage. We also received extra money for the use of our personal vehicles. It was enough then to pay for gas for the day plus a little extra towards maintenance, like brake pads and oil changes. But we had no hope of going full time with benefits.

The job was so good that there were more people who wanted to work than there were jobs available. When the management decided that they wanted to hire a friend or relative (or friend or relative of a politician), someone had to quit or be fired to make an opening.

It's hard to fire people who do their job well. So the next step was for management to make the employee so miserable that he or she would quit. Supervisors and postmasters would yell, scream and cuss at people—usually for no good reason. They would load the employee down with impossible workloads. They would demand extra work outside the rural craft. I know people who were given disciplinary letters for stealing postal equipment (rubber bands on the car floor), going to the bathroom too many times, and for not being able to work a 12-hour route in eight hours. Then there was sabotage. Tires would "lose" air, radio antennas were broken off, and dings and scratches appeared on our personal vehicles.

I'm glad to say that once we "scrubs" were allowed to join the rural carrier union, our work environment changed. And sad to say it took the postal massacres to force management to pay attention to hostile work environments.

When it was my turn to be under pressure to quit I had a simple strategy. I wrote myself a note and folded it into a small square. When the supervisor screamed at me (usually for mistakes made on days I wasn't working) I would take the note out of my pocket and slowly unfold it. I would read the note then slowly refold it and replace it in my pocket. If the yelling got really ugly, I might repeat this process a couple of times.

The note was simple. The note was a message

from me to myself to simply: KEEP YOUR DAMN
MOUTH SHUT!!!

Antiques

Some of the mail we receive for our routes comes wrapped in plastic, strings and plastic ties. We open these bundles with scissors or knives to put the individual mail in route order. I used a pair of scissors I had brought from home when I first started with the postal service.

The United States Postal Service, in its wisdom, decided to remove all sharp objects from the post office. They told us to untie or use our fingernails to tear plastic. Of course we filed a grievance and after a few weeks we won.

Our "sharp objects" had been put into a tub in the postmaster's office. When I went to get my scissors they were gone. I was furious. My supervisor told me to just pick a different pair. My scissors had been removed from my work area when I was not present and by damn I wanted them back. Mine were really good scissors and everything left in the tub was junk.

I told my supervisor that my scissors were valuable antiques. He asked why I had antique scissors anyway. I told him they were old when I brought them to the post office and that was over 25 years ago.

My scissors appeared on my desk the next day. Nobody confessed to taking them. I did get picked on about my antiqueness.

The Name of the Beer Joint

One of my coworkers asked me if I delivered a certain street by the highway. When I said yes, he wanted to know the name of the nightclub on that road. I told him they didn't have a mailbox so I'd never paid attention. It was slightly back from the road and closed when I delivered that street. He asked me to look and tell him the next day. So I did.

There was only one sign on the building so I told my coworker the name.

Michelob.

Puzzle Parcel

When a parcel is too large for a customer's mailbox, we usually leave it by the door. Exceptions would be if the customer has requested that we not leave parcels at the house, there is nowhere to leave it safe from weather, or if there is an aggressive dog. The company that sent the parcel can give permission to leave the parcel at a residence.

On rare occasions, a mail carrier can be required to pay for a damaged parcel. If the customer has requested in writing to not have parcels left outside of the box and a parcel is then stolen or damaged, the carrier can be liable. With one exception.

My coworker had this happen. He left a large parcel by the front door of a customer who didn't want parcels left outside of the box. The customer's new dog (that my coworker didn't know about) shredded the parcel. They gathered up all the tiny pieces for evidence, brought them to the post office and demanded payment. My coworker spent a considerable amount of time reassembling the parcel. He found the important three inches of the address and did not have to purchase the parcel.

Any mail we deliver has two customers: the one we deliver to and the one who originally sent the mail. My coworker found the information that the parcel sender had requested.

The instructions read: Carrier Leave If No Response. The sender replaced the parcel for the customer.

Straps

Mail carriers don't spend all our time riding around in trucks. We spend several hours of each day preparing the mail for delivery. We "case" the mail in route order and then "pull down," put it in a gurney, and load our trucks. Some carriers use trays and some use straps.

Rubber bands are an essential part of this process. Before using rubber bands, we used short leather straps to tie bundles of mail in bunches. They were replaced with longer nylon straps that hold a bigger bundle. Trays are replacing them. The post office is gradually phasing out the straps in favor of trays. I like the straps.

The straps were intended only for bundling mail. But some of the old-timers discovered different uses. Mr. G was particularly clever in his. He drove a beat-up Oldsmobile and it was literally falling apart. He used his straps to hold his trunk down, his muffler up and his battery on. His straps became muddy and had acid holes in them.

When the straps would wear out, management would replace them. They told Mr. G that he would have to buy his own. Instead, he would sneak his yucky straps in other carrier's bags and take their good straps. Then that carrier would trade them with someone else.

Mr. G has been retired for many years now but those nasty straps are still out there making the rounds.

Competition Pays

I delivered mail in a city that was rapidly expanding. My route grew so fast that we split it to make a new route. I gave up almost three hundred boxes and gained that number back in a year. Other carriers would brag that they had added six or seven new boxes in a week. When they asked me, I told them I had added a new subdivision that week. I was always tired.

My new subdivision was full of twisty turns and dead end cul-de-sacs. One day I noticed a competitor driving round and round. He pulled up to me and admitted he was lost. I tried to explain the convoluted path but he just got more confused. We were both running late so I suggested a plan. He laughed and agreed. For the price of four stamps, I delivered his parcel for him.

Ice Breakers

Working as a mail carrier in southern Mississippi, weather conditions can be extreme. Extreme heat, tornados, flash floods and hurricanes can stress a postal worker. And the customers don't always understand that crossing a flooded road to get to their mailbox isn't really a good idea, or that when the engine overheats the mail will be late that day, or that tornados are terrifying.

Snow and ice are rare but do happen. The old-timers told us to bring something to break the ice from the mailboxes so they could be opened. I remembered that advice, but the carriers who didn't had to improvise. They used a shoe and got a cold foot.

I confess I found it a little therapeutic to whack some of the mailboxes with my small hammer.

Testing the Waters

Many rural postal customers run small businesses out of their homes or their vehicles. Plumbers and shade tree mechanics, writers and palm readers, caterers and house cleaners, pet sitters and painters are just a few. One customer collected china. At a sale, she would get a set of china that was missing a few dishes. She would find them online and fill in the set. Then she would sell the complete set for more money.

An unusual business for one of my customers was a water-testing lab. People would send my customer frozen water in small boxes or ice chests all wrapped up in plastic and tape. She would joke about atomic wastewater and monster bacteria. She grew her business until she was getting hundreds in a week and I forgot about what was in them. Until the spill.

On that hot day, the ice chest didn't have all the

plastic and tape. When I reached to pull the parcel from the back seat, the latch snapped, the lid slipped and water sloshed over me. Then I remembered mutant microbiology and radiation. My face must have shown what I was thinking because the customer quickly reassured me that the water was for a fluoride test.

I guess she was telling the truth because that was years ago and I'm still not a ninja turtle.

Honesty

Years ago, I took a sociology class in college. One day when we came into the room there was a ten-dollar bill on a desk. We students came into the room and took our seats. The professor was unusually late so we waited. Finally a girl got up, bounced over to the money and pocketed it. Then the professor came in.

He mentioned the money and the girl spoke up loudly that she had taken it. Her excuse was if someone was dumb enough to leave it there then they deserved to lose it. We had a lively class discussion.

The professor asked each of us why we didn't take the money. When it was my turn I told him that while I didn't know who the money belonged to, I knew exactly who it didn't belong to, and that was me. He pointed at me and said I had earned an A for the day.

My dad is an honest person. He worked for the post office for 24 years, as a clerk and then as a rural carrier. I was telling him about the time my customers left their utility money, in cash, in their stamp envelope by accident. They were very happy when I showed up at the door to ask if they really wanted hundreds of stamps.

Dad laughed and said he could trump that. He had a customer who worked from home and often mailed magazine-sized envelopes. Dad opened the mailbox to a large stack and was thumbing through to check for postage when he found something that didn't belong.

It was a $100,000 bearer bond. The customer was very happy to get that back.

Part Five. Everything Else

Not the Mail

These are some of the things I've found in mailboxes that weren't mail:

Rabbit poop (at a politician's address).

Firecrackers, new and used.

Newspapers and parcels from competitors. (Not allowed.)

Live animals: chickens, lizards, bugs, green snakes, frogs, birds with nests, kittens.

Not-live animals: a rattlesnake, lizards, frogs, skunk, a kitten.

Wasp nest.

Cold drink on a hot day from a customer.

Candy bar in a bowl of ice from the same nice customer.

Gun.

Cash.

Keys.

Beer can.

Christmas presents—sometimes for me!

Superstitious Mail Carriers

It is bad luck to kill lizards and frogs in a mailbox.

Never, ever run over a turtle.

Mail bundles or trays are numbered. It is bad luck to end the numbers on 13. Use 12 1/2 or skip to 14.

Do not say out loud that tomorrow will be a better day.

Never, ever say that things could be worse.

Postal Language

Day sleepers: people on night shift who have requested not to be disturbed.

Dead box: mailbox that is not currently receiving mail for at least 90 days.

Sleeper: a piece of mail that gets pushed to the back of the sorting case. We check for these every day.

Hot case: a sorting case where all carriers make last-minute checks for resorted mail before leaving for their routes. Usually painted red.

Current resident: the person who lives at an address *now*!

Box holder: generic address for the owner of a mailbox.

Dead heading: when a carrier loops back on his or her route and passes mailboxes already served.

Accountable mail: this is mail that the carrier

signs for personally.

Certified: mail that has to be signed for by an adult at the address.

Registered: mail that is kept locked up until delivery.

Call for mail: extra-charge service for backdoor pickup before business.

COD: cash on delivery.

POV: personally owned vehicle.

Bad Addresses

These are addresses that mail carriers received— and delivered:

Third house on left after school.

House by the railroad with the blue shed.

Uncle Harold (no street).

First house before the railroad tracks.

Big yellow house.

Granny Jones (no street).

House on the gravel road with the outhouse.

No Good Deeds...

One Christmas Eve, I walked a parcel (obviously a present for the baby) up a rutted, impassable driveway. Now, instead of fixing their road, they think I should do that every time.

I saw an elderly customer lying in the road and helped her get home. Her daughter tried to sue the Post Office.

I picked up a "lost" dog and returned him home. His owner had actually given him away. Twice.

I have a few mailboxes that don't have lids. When it rains I wrap the mail in Wal-Mart plastic bags. This is not a requirement. When I don't work the subs don't do this and the customer calls in a complaint.

A carrier I knew saw an accident on a four-lane highway across the median. He called for help and then waited for help to arrive. When the emergency people came, the driver told them my coworker caused the accident.

Murphy Was a Mailman

Murphy's Law at the post office:

On a day you need to get off early, the delivery point system mail will have two sets of addressed box holders. This means you have to stop at every box.

Rainy day parcels: the day that the majority of the parcels will not fit in the mailbox. And it rains.

The day my soldier daughter comes home from a war zone and I have a flat tire and the jack breaks.

A day that the mail is light and you could skip some mailboxes but all the flags are up, indicating outgoing mail.

A nice customer leaves you homemade cookies in the box but ants find them before you do.

Beautiful Day to Be a Mail Carrier

I work outside in the sunshine and it is a beautiful day the Lord has made.

Storming and there is a flash flood warning on the weather alert but it is a beautiful day the Lord has made.

Hailing, but I only got a few dings and one small crack on the windshield before I got under the huge live oak tree. And it is a beautiful day the Lord has made.

Rain, freezing and the mailboxes are iced closed but it is still a beautiful day the Lord has made.

It is very hot and I can hear the rubber bands that hold the bundles of mail popping as they melt. Yes, it is a beautiful day the Lord has made.

The sky is blue, the winds are cool... and it is a beautiful day the Lord has made!

THE LAUGHING POSTMAN

Afterword

Whispers

Every day, God whispers something to me. I don't always listen.

One day on my mail route I heard the whisper. Stop. Look. I pulled off the road. I looked.

When Hurricane Katrina swept through this area years ago, it knocked down a small grove of pecan trees. But they did not die.

With the trees' red-clay-covered roots exposed, and the trunks parallel to the ground, they did not give up and die.

Now, years later the branches of the trees reach up and up, giving shade to cattle and fruit for a new generation.

God wanted me to know that even if events in my life knock me down, I don't have to give up. I can thrive as I am. Thank you Lord, for the whispers.

PREVIEW OF: THE LAUGHING

POSTMAN REDELIVERS

The Great Bill Escape

Part of my mail route was on a four-lane highway. Traffic was usually bad but on this day roadwork was making it horrendous. Cars would let me dodge in and out of the barely moving line. And to top it off it was a windy, blustery day.

I was reaching out with several pieces of mail to put in a mailbox when a gust of wind ripped the letters from my hand. I got out of my truck and picked up the mail. Except for one small, thin, postcard-sized letter.

The last letter acted like a miniature kite. Every time I thought I had it the darn thing would flitter away. Finally I managed to put my foot on it and pick it up.

When I turned back to my truck someone beeped a horn in a congratulatory way. I realized that I had been the momentary amusement for the stalled traffic.

There was nothing else I could do. I raised the letters in a two-fisted winner's salute—and got lots of happy horn blowing.

Tarred and Feathered

My grandfather was a rural carrier. In the latter years of his life after he was long retired and I was just beginning my career, we would compare stories of postal life.

In his time, people would mail order almost anything. While I have delivered baby chicks in boxes on a regular basis, he would have full-grown chickens in slated crates. And if it was a cold day, he would keep them in the cab of his truck.

Pawpaw also had to apply glue to stamps to make them stick to letters and he had a small scale to determine weight. The glue was in a jar with a dabber attached to the lid.

One cold spring day, he had two full-grown roosters in one wire crate to deliver. Yes, two roosters, one cage. They fought and feathers flew.

He was driving a bumpy gravel road and his glue

jar bounced opened. Glue spilled. Everywhere. It got on him, all over the inside of his truck and on the mail.

Feathers and glue. While driving with the window down.

Singing in the Rain

Sometimes letter carriers are in a world of our own. On some routes I've worked, most of the customers were not home during the week and I could work hours without seeing a person. Dogs, yes, but no customers. Just me and the mailboxes.

On one memorable rainy day I was serving a row of twelve boxes. I had my favorite radio station on and it was playing oldies from my high school days. I was happily singing along with the Eagles when I heard someone clear his throat.

Embarrassed, I stopped singing and looked at the customer; he was holding an umbrella, waiting for his mail.

"Can I help you, sir?" I asked.

"Yes," he replied, smiling. "Don't quit your day job."

Exuberant Bulldogs

I have a customer who loves dogs. Because this customer also loves eBay and Amazon, I made it my business to befriend these dogs when they were puppies. Three large Dobermans, one Great Dane, one very short and wide Bassett Hound and a half-grown pure white English bulldog live at this address. They all love me. And my treats (given with permission).

One rainy day, I had parcels for this customer. The adult dogs waited on the dry porch with doggy dignity. As I placed the parcel by the door and turned back to my truck, I saw the young bulldog running towards me from the barn. He wasn't pure white today. This large healthy puppy had a tendency for full body contact so I braced for impact. I'm thinking *muddy dog*.

The smell reached me just as he leaped. I turned

sideways and avoided the full body blow. I yelled, "Bad dog!" and he dropped like a flat frog.

I cleaned up at a gas station but the smell lingered all day. It wasn't mud the white dog had rolled in but cow manure.

Christmas Gifts

Someone recently asked me what my favorite Christmas gift from a mail customer was. I had skipped a couple of meals that day so my first thought was about food.

Over the years I have received some yummy presents. Some of the most memorable are hot chocolate and warm banana nut bread on a cold icy day, smoked ham, cookies, divinity (my favorite!), frozen Snickers bars and ice water on a hot day and more cookies. Christmas cards and nice notes are always appreciated and brighten my day.

This is my favorite Christmas gift. I received an ordinary glass ornament with wiggly writing that said #1 Mail Carrier. I gave the customer a thank-you note and put the ornament on my tree. The next year, I was personally handed my ornament by the now-first grader. The writing wasn't so wiggly and again proclaimed me #1 Mail Carrier. The third year the ornament said #1 Mail Lady! As the years went by, the ornaments got more decorative with glitter and stickers.

I still have most of those inexpensive glass ornaments. They are precious to me.

"Cheeky" Mail Carrier

I delivered mail in a rural area that was in the process of becoming a high-end gated community. The streets were laid out in winding artistic loops with the idea of having as much lakefront property as possible. This made for lots of dead end cul-de-sacs.

I discovered that bumping into the curbs to serve the boxes in these tight circles was destroying the sidewalls on my tires. This was expensive.

I asked the customers to move the problem boxes a few feet to solve the problem and all but one did. He told me, in a nasal English accent, that he liked his box where it was. I explained the problem with my tires but he just shrugged.

With my supervisor's permission I curtailed delivery of his mail. This infuriated the man. He waylaid me and proceeded to rant, rave and cuss.

Exasperated, I told him, "Fine! You sit in your car

on the passenger side, drive with your left foot and hand and if you can serve the box without running up the curb I will resume your mail delivery!"

He called my postmaster and claimed I had been rude and "cheeky." The postmaster told him my idea sounded good and he should try it.

Two days later the mailbox was moved. And my coworkers had a fine time calling me the "cheeky" carrier.

BC (Before Cell Phones)

When cell phones first came out they were large, bulky things that came in a lunch-box sized bag. I had a friend working for the new mobile phone company and she asked me to give her business card to my coworkers.

My fellow carriers and I decided the newfangled phone was just some gadget or fad that would soon pass. One of the old-timers laughed at me and threw his card in the garbage.

The next week, that old-timer witnessed a motorcycle wreck and saved a young man's life by applying a tourniquet. The carrier told me he would have given anything for that bag phone in those bloody long moments before help arrived.

Within a few weeks, every rural carrier in my office owned one of those "bag phones."

The Naked Truth Two

When I first started as a mail carrier, my coworkers filled my ears with unbelievable stories. Dogs climbing in the windows, naked people answering the door, invites for big country lunches and many more. Over the next thirty years all that has happened. And more.

My second naked mail customer was an elderly man. He lived at the end of a long driveway and his was the only house in sight. I had a parcel for him and beeped the horn to let him know I was there. He was walking around the corner of his house as I was getting out of my truck. I jumped back in the truck! He didn't have a stitch of clothing on.

He was very matter of fact. It was "too hot for clothes." I had him sign for the parcel, carefully keeping my eyes on his face. Then I drove to the next house on my route.

His son laughed when I told him. "Dad did it again!"

Well, it really *was* hot that day.

Duct Taped

Providing a proper mail receptacle is the responsibility of the customer. Whether to accept that mailbox is up to the carrier. Most mailboxes are purchased from a store but some are handmade. If they are watertight and safe to open and close, I'm OK with them. Once the carrier places mail in a box that mailbox is considered approved. To stop delivery after that requires an act of the postmaster or a supervisor.

One household on my route had its mailbox crushed, most likely by an eighteen-wheeler cutting the curve too sharp. I took the mail to the house to let them know about the demise of their mailbox. They told me it would be replaced soon. The next day, a cheap plastic mailbox was loosely nailed to a post. Inside was a note saying that a better mailbox would be up by the weekend. So I delivered.

Several weekends later, the box had not been improved. Instead, the nails holding the box to the post had worked loose and the mailbox would fall off when I shut the lid. I left a nice note asking the customer to please secure the mailbox to the post. The next day I stopped several feet before the box. I couldn't believe what I was seeing.

Someone had used an entire industrial-sized roll of duct tape on the mailbox to hold it to the post. Starting about halfway up the post and wrapping over the middle of the box, the shining silver tape engulfed the mailbox. Even the flag had a star-shaped duct tape cover.

I laughed and put the mail in the box.

Rear View Mirrors

My dad worked for the United States Post Office for twenty-four years. He had retired from the Marine Corps with twenty years and gone to college on the GI bill. After taking the postal exam (he scored in the upper 90s) he got work as a clerk/carrier. My dad worked as a clerk, supervisor, temporary postmaster (officer in charge) and finally as a rural carrier in a very small town. He liked the last job the best.

He told me this story. His mail route was over a hundred miles long with lots of washed out gravel roads and one-lane roads. He had only a few hundred mail customers because most of his route was National Forest. And it was a log truck, he told me, that almost killed him.

Rear view mirrors are a wonderful invention. We mail carriers depend on all three mirrors for pulling in and out of traffic as we serve our mailboxes. My dad was serving a mailbox at the bottom of a hill when he looked in the rear view mirror and saw a fully loaded log truck topping the hill. In the oncoming traffic was a van. Thinking quickly, my dad punched the accelerator and went in the ditch. The truck managed to stop further down the road and the driver walked back to help my dad get his car out of the ditch. The van kept going.

"I'm really glad you got out of the way," the driver told my dad. "I knew I couldn't stop. Figured the van might have kids so I decided if I had to hit someone it was going to be you."

I hope whoever invented rear view mirrors is rich.

Afterword

To My Readers

I hope you enjoyed this double volume of The Laughing Postman—and the bonus material. My email address is thelaughingpostman@gmail.com. I welcome comments and hope you will leave a review on Amazon.

A special thanks to my Facebook friends for all the comments and "likes." I post my stories on the Facebook group page: yes, you guessed it, The Laughing Postman.

Special Thanks

Thanks to Cathy Sellers for the proofreading and editing and the encouraging words.

Big thanks to Janet Mayo for listening and laughing and nagging me to finish.

Made in the USA
Charleston, SC
28 June 2016